White Monkeys

POEMS BY
BIN RAMKE

Athens
The University of Georgia Press

Copyright © 1981 by the University of Georgia Press
Athens, Georgia 30602

Set in 10 on 12 point Monticello type
Printed in the United States of America

Library of Congress Cataloging in Publication Data

Ramke, Bin, 1947–
  White monkeys.
   I. Title.
PS3568.A446W5   811'.54   80-24582
ISBN 0-8203-0544-8
ISBN 0-8203-0551-0 (pbk.)

The publication of this book is supported by a grant from the
National Endowment for the Arts, a federal agency.

for Nicolas,
his dear, blond head

Acknowledgments

The author and the publisher gratefully acknowledge the following publications in which poems in this volume first appeared.

The Agni Review: "The Magician," "Sex Therapy"
Georgia Review: "Eclipse," "The Concert for Bangladesh," "*Mater dolorosa*," "Projection: Milk and Memory," "Parabolic"
New Arts: "*Paysage moralisé*," "Pleasures of the Flesh," "Drive-in"
The New Yorker: "The Obscure Pleasure of the Indistinct" © 1978 by The New Yorker Magazine, Inc.
Ohio Review: "Westminster Chimes," "Foreign Language," "Circus" under the title "Festival," "On Living the Rich, Full Life"
Plum: "The Petting Zoo," "The Late Show"
Poetry: "Victory Drive, Near Fort Benning, Georgia," "Obscurantism," "The Object of the Dispute" © 1979 by the Modern Poetry Association
Southern Poetry Review: "The Dangers of the Domestic"
Southern Review: "Rose Hill Shopping Center"
Stump I: "Widow"
Vision: "Why He Wants to Sleep Near Water," "Nuns in Sunshine"

Contents

I

Westminster Chimes   3
Märchen   4
Eclipse   6
The Magician   8
Myocardial Infarction, and Other Attacks of the Heart   9
Paysage moralisé   12
Why I Am Afraid to Have Children   14
White Monkeys   15
The Concert for Bangladesh   18
Theme and Variation:
      Abbeville, Louisiana / Blanco County, Texas   21
Parabolic   25
Projection: Milk and Memory   26
Nostalgia   28

II

Obscurantism   31
The Object of the Dispute   32
Breakfast in the Suburbs   36
Sex Therapy   37
Victory Drive, Near Fort Benning, Georgia   43
Georgia   44
The Obscure Pleasure of the Indistinct   45
On Living the Rich, Full Life   46
Circus   47
Rose Hill Shopping Center   53
The Late Show   61
The Petting Zoo   63
Butterflies, Late Fall: Nostalgia   64

III

Mater Dolorosa   67
Rain   69
What to Do Till the Doctor Comes   71
Drive-in   72
The Dangers of the Domestic   73
Foreign Language   74
Saint Anthony Confronts Sodomy in the New World   76
Nuns in Sunshine   77
Why He Wants to Sleep Near Water   80
Widow   81
Three Views of One Woman   82
What We Learned to Do to Each Other   85
The Rape of the Divorcée's Sisters   86
Pleasures of the Flesh   89
Evening Seduction Scene with Telescope   90
The Desire for a Mediterranean Sea   92
Travelogue   94

I

Westminster Chimes

We are moved to memory: it is,
after all, spring. After white days,
not of, in this southern state, snow,
but of frost internalized,
of cold incipience.

I lean into the white waltz
of birds across the evening sky,
I remember a child I was,
and see him at a window
listening to the whippoorwills
call across a dreary field
which glistens in last light,
orange. He lived there
and loved the world.

I hear a chime from town
strike the hour—after all,
it's spring and all windows
open—a beat behind the clock
in the living room. Nine,
my old bed time.

Suddenly nothing
can keep me from sleep.

Märchen

Once up on time dreams fly
out the window, morning
grins, the sun's over the rim—
day starts. The little father
does his best: sons run
circles around him. He smiles.
The flowers of the dogwood
hang, past their season, white
as three stars in the evening.
Evening cool and drinks:
a son remembers his father,
his father's funeral, the last
long look.

No. He is not dead
this time. Sons will
have their jokes. Clever
sons are not always
happiest. His mother
loved him but father
knew better.

Three stars
hang silver in the dawn
over the Pawnshop.
Carry any remnant of a father—
once pawned a time
cannot return.

A man died and the family
found a pawn check in his wallet:
from Poland, they guessed,
or some such never-never land.

Eclipse

Recall the light
that moved under the bedroom door,
that sifted through the dust-mice caught
beneath the bed, then was gone.
It was your mother in the hall,
deep in the night—the sound of water
from the bathroom, the whine of plumbing
like the torturer's bride escaped
into the wall.

*

I could not turn
away from their flash when distant
visiting relatives took pictures:
I stared at the blue bulbs
they licked then stuck in steel
sockets. Afterward, the seared spot
still floating in my eye,
I would secretly peel the plastic
coating off—a safety device,
they told me, in case the glass globe
should explode.

*

My father held
the black, nearly opaque sheets for me
to protect my eyes, he said, but that
I would remember this eclipse forever.

The papers carried stories of two boys
gone blind from unprotected staring.
They should have had such a father
as mine, I said, but wondered
what it was like, that last moment
of sun, that ring of corrosive light
just at that moment beyond recall.

This flower, jasmine, old-
ivory-colored, climbed
the porch posts for fifty years.
Each blossom in miniature,
a child's toy—you would not
believe such a thing did not
come from a hand and sharp knife.

And azaleas—too many
for a farm where land should go
to money crops—could have been
folded tissue, the after school
handiwork of a hundred
Southern daughters.

And cockscomb, and bougainvillea,
and snapdragon, and morning glory,
and butterfly lily, and scarlet
runner, and scarlet pimpernel
which closed in bad weather.

*

But now we live in suburbs, and no one
is a farmer. Yet we are proud
of our plum trees, and rhododendrons
when they survive the winter.
We cross each other's lawns at sunset
exchanging words and cuttings.

10

I, for instance, don't sleep near
a river, and in the evening I have
no rock where I sit to smoke and listen
to calls of birds giving warning,
though I have noticed a note of mourning
from trucks on the interstate,
and the airplanes crossing
above my apartment seem to signal
something in green and red.

(I wake some mornings reaching
for the last dream, this kind:
from a bus you catch a glimpse of a woman
you loved but she is still young,
wears white and laughs as she turns
the corner. So finally two blocks away
you stand on the street wondering
which way to turn and whether
they'll notice you late at the office.)

        *

                    Sunlight
through a screen door; the red
linoleum warm to the touch,
oh, old: something Etruscan
in the look of it, the red of it;
a cut flower on the table, the first
from her garden, and the slow
shuffle of slippered feet.

11

Paysage moralisé

1

A figure at a farther reach
stumbles against the sky,
then straightens to descend
over the horizon home.

There remain in the backyard
only the children, filthiest
beasts of the field, sad
in self-knowledge, waiting
to be called to dinner,
to sit in wonder then
to be sent to bed.

Finally the stars wheel up
through the limbs
of elms to shine precisely
on the round edge of the water glass.

2

A small child sees the stars
waver, reflected
in his glass. He is sick,
has missed six days of school.
He tries to put the glass back
on the nightstand—he was thirsty
when wakened by the dream—
and lets it fall. He hears

his mother's advancing step
on the wide stair.

3

He has always loved saints.
He makes dolls of flowers
and dried grass, and gives them
names: Saint Aloysius,
because no mother names
a son for him;
Sebastian because it's fun
to push the broom straw
arrows in;

Ignatius Loyola because
he had a limp;
Saint John Bosco because
he was only a boy.

On an afternoon in May
he read of Saint Venantius
who was only fifteen,
and saw his lovely head
lopped off while the Emperor
slouched past the door distracted
by the glorious evening star.

Why I Am Afraid to Have Children

A morning like others, and a father
stood there, black against the light.
The screen of the door buckled softly
in brief wind, the morning heat
already rising.

This ground never made anyone rich,
least of all this father. So his job was in town
and he didn't know how sad he was playing
with his toy farm, paying for it.

I didn't know. I was a child
as small as I would ever be. It is
only a memory, a ragged edge,
and perhaps meaningless. A spindly morning glory
glowed the only spot of color
over his shoulder.

White Monkeys

1

"But if we are asked what purpose the *history
of a monstrous nature can serve*, we will answer:
to pass from the prodigies of nature's *deviations*
to the marvels of *art*."
                    —from D'Alembert's
Preliminary Discourse to the Encyclopedia of Diderot

2

On my desk I keep a bisque monkey
whose sad face yellows with time:
I recall a long line of toys, and walks
with relatives along small rivers; all men
grow only in small ways
only older.

3

What memory cannot provide
is a barbarism of the moment.
I picked the passionflower
along the banks of a muddy ditch
dangerous enough to drown small boys:

the flower is less a marvel now,
the ditch less deep.

4

At night while white moths fluttered
against old screens
cousins told stories
which only we youngest believed:
animals in the far woods,
the vestige of bear which still
might rise against the smell
of man; owls gigantic
in the night which might
develop a taste for child;
snakes in time of high water
filling the front porch.

I do not recall that in that time
we ever (most difficult
of earthly tasks) slept.

5

We saw "The Time Machine"
at our local library—three adults
in a room dark with children.
Some had come in a single line,
had quietly followed themselves
out of the state's asylum.
While the normal children screamed
at the glowing eyes of Morlocks,
while the normal children cringed
at the monster's decomposing face,

not used to the compressions
of time and movie-making,
these straight-line children nodded
a solemn yes: that is how it was,
that is how it will be. All
was still order in their
most logical world, all well.

6

I walked the pebbled paths of zoos
from Houston to San Diego, from Seattle
to Boston. And if you ask what I remember
I will tell you: an albino snake, rare
as a glimpse of snowflake on the thumbnail,
and a glimpse of white in the monkey trees.

The Concert for Bangladesh

Watch out now, take care, beware
                                    —Leon Russell

We not only gagged on the lima beans
but wept in the gravy listening
to our mother's stories of the starving
and our own unconscionable luck.

The limacine trail of fat in our plates
reflected the last of sun from the windows:
the last moments of afternoon wasted,
and the added insult of dishes to do.

We brothers believed deeply
in God and malnutrition, saw
no conflict there, took on
the burden of cold beans
and indigestible liver.

And to the Jewish question: How
will you help the poor
when you are grown? we answered well:
become a missionary, be good
to their pets, give milk-money;

but our sister was showered with tears
and nickels when she said—Hope
there will be no poor
when I am grown.

*

18

What *is* the burden? To give
at the office? To weave a coat,
motley as Joseph's, of guilt?
To drive an old car?

*

And last week we drove, both of us grown
in some ways, at least older,
through the farmland of south Georgia.
I loved the pigs, sighing for mud—

and the wide-bred cows,
freely fed and freely feeding.
And you saw, for the first time,
sorghum, knife-edged, honing
under slow rain:

but do you remember the sunflower field
waving heavy under rain
along the road to Florida?
It is, I am told, a money crop
especially suited for export.

But do you recall the yellow edge,
and how each bloom, languid
in gray mist, shivered?
Acres of them, and the rift
of road continued to Florida.

19

And the bossed blooms,
the few a foot or more
above the rest, big as umbrellas,
with seed centers dark
as the sky they hung sullenly from?

Theme and Variation:
Abbeville, Louisiana / Blanco County, Texas,
1957–1977

My God, my own son would be forbidden
    to play there, among
the hammer and tongs, the forge and the forest
    of angle-iron, the heat

and the heroic sweat. I adored it
    and them, their size,
and the grit in my creased neck.
    I picked spit

flowers of tobacco from the floor. I ranged
    the wrenches on their bench,
swept the shavings neatly beneath
    the vice and heard

the hiss of drawknife slice hickory
    with sleek precision.
My uncle was his father's boy, big
    and owner of the shop.

His sons were in their own ways big,
    short but wide—
and fine feeders all. They played
    their symphony

long through a summer afternoon
    and I the only audience,
the only lowly lover of their wretched
    racket. No school, I

was given variation, change of routine
    and the purity of mindless
muscle as reward for arithmetic:
    the beautiful dust floor.

Through the doors of the shop the heat
    opened into sunlight:
they sent me, crossing carefully
    such dangers as streets,

with nickels for *pop rouge.* I counted
    the lizards hung
on barbed wire by the butcher bird,
    notes on a staff, a music

of *this* sphere: the pale hearts impaled
    with alacrity, with no regret,
with reason: the bird provides
    for a narrow future.

The men drank noisily as if cursing
    while muttering dark
jokes about women—they looked,
    laughed, turned

the glittering bottles through the air
    into the corner crashing.

    *

And in the evening when the sun angled
    through beams searching
for an honest face, I considered heaven
    a huge barn of a shop

infested with rats like virtue. Sparks
    from the forge and electric
arc welder pulsed with purpose into night;
    the shimmer of late work

and the bare bulb illuminating paper
    piled like snow
on the black roll-top desk—three
    generations at least

of other men's bills. The day tempered hard
    orange to black of wrought iron.

    *

Nothing remains: there is such danger
    in the world you would
not believe unless you believe in God.
    He's dead and his sons

run a business for oil companies, renting
    men and machines
who fly across the borders of Louisiana
    in helicopters.

23

His shop became a family museum
    to a man killed
in a fast car on the way to Texas
    to hunt deer on his toy

ranch. His pet cows, strange breeds
    whose names no one
now remembers, also outlived him.
    Only they are patient

with no memories, awaiting at feed time
    the approaching ranch hand's
        impetuous hymn.

Parabolic

Light attaches to the gravel of the drive
As if hawked from a throat—an unpleasant
Time of day this time of year, wet, cold.
He leaves for work in his blue car coughing,
Reminding him of needs: a tune-up, a gift
For his wife's birthday, a dental appointment.

What is such a scene to you? A man
Or two leaves a wife or two and no
bird sings, or stops; nor heart, necessarily.

Light glitters from the mica flecks of the drive
As if struck again flinty in a cave—the pleasant
Sound of morning rain reminds him, as
He leaves for work in his blue car resisting,
Of the wish for simpler needs: firewood, shoes
For the horse, bulbs to simmer till spring in a hillside.

But who, this time of mortal fury, cares
For your small, smaller visions, noose of
Nothing beyond the simpering edge, bright threshold
        of "grandpa's farm"?

Light crashes from stone, stark; crunch under
His car in the blue thunderous morning; flickers
Cross the controls as he backs out, cold.
He leaves for work in his blue car dreading,
Trying to forget such needs: a wife, a child,
A long line of ancestors calling him home.

Projection: Milk and Memory
for Richard Howard

He wanted to make maps, shiny
Surfaces of mountain, marsh, man-mixed
Cityscapes of streets, escapes beyond
Himself. He studied maps looking
For the trap, the fictional cul-de-sac
Cartographers include to protect
Copyright. He found three by age ten.

There was always rain streaming the windows
Of the nursery when we had cakes and milk—
Small bitter cakes, always with almond,
And always Ellen would make wet circles
On her papers, though she was kind
And had green eyes. But I continued
Studying maps under the warm yellow
Of the lamp, even at three in the long
Afternoon as vague, misted shadows
Crossed the privets, the hawthorns,
The crushed granite walks and borders
Of delphinium that grained the long
North side of the west wing.
I drank my milk carefully
Not daring to spill a drop
On the vast green lawn of blotter.

Figure-ground relationships: whether
The zebra in the alphabet book
Is black with white stripes
Or white with black bands. Littoral
Meanings on maps are delicate

Scratch of pin point tracing the band
Of land and water lushest with fish,
Fattest with mystery and change.

So the days went by and we grew
Full of significance together. Sister
Lovelier and lovelier. Her hands filled
Themselves with air as she talked,
The shape of silver vases, crystal
Carved, or paperweights. Cunning.
And she began to point her toes—
Habit from dancing class that morning—
Just thus, and fill the carpet with meaning.
But there was a stain where
She threw the inkpot, petulant
At geography, full of remorse
Though she may now be, living
In her fair foreign country.

Nostalgia

I did not grow up among paintings.
We had calendars on the kitchen wall
And a portrait of poor Jesus, but I remember
A picture, a calendar above my bed,
October, I suppose, a picture of trees
Turned gold in autumn. I was a schoolboy
Home sick; I stared for hours through
Long afternoons while mother cleaned
Around me or cooked beans and chicken;
I entered it as she listened to the radio's
Romance of Helen Trent. I walked
Myself down a trail littered with gold,
I felt the crispness of cold like you
Feel the crushed ice of daiquiris
Against the tongue. You understand I was
A small boy in south Texas who knew nothing
Of autumn leaves, of winter, or of art.

II

Obscurantism

This is the dust which passes
from breath to breath,
from eye to eye. In New Orleans
a man brings his daughter
to the park. They buy balloons.
They feed the crusts
of a picnic to the ducks.

Later she will disappoint him,
marry, and have dirty children
who drive powerful cars
and park on the marigolds.

Sometimes even now he sits
in bars. He smiles at the stripper
who wears glasses. It makes her
human, somehow. She is blond
and thin, and has a child
in Chicago. She does not
miss him so much anymore, she says.

The Object of the Dispute

It is Margaret you mourn for

1

The day closes its circle; another
night without mercy. The shell
on the desk becomes a necessary
object, a thing

to contemplate while the children
sleep: it is glossy with spots.
On the beach his daughters
collected shells, turned them

in their small, creased palms,
asked appropriate questions.
What other husks will they handle

before they're through?
Already they take pleasure
in his gathering patina of years.

2

Margaret, the youngest, said
simple things, thus was never
understood: like
there is a tree; or, there

is a flower. He was a father
but did not trust his daughter
although he knew it was a tree;
or, he knew it really

was a flower.
We must have faith, she
told him, that sometimes
things are what they seem.

She did not really tell him that,
it only seemed so, as in a dream.

3

Margaret, the youngest, returned
three books to the library. Evening,
and slow birds made, in her sight,
spirals ascending, like looking

down the rifling of a barrel.
One was an old novel, quiet,
full of nights in front of glowing
coals, of the hiss of gas lamps;

one was a book of birds, their colors,
calls, and all their small
catastrophes; the last was a book

of prophecy: returning it for
her father, she sneaked, walking,
a look at Sex in Samoa.

4

Margaret, the youngest, watched
an airplane in the night signal
something red and green: she dreamed,
as daughters will, the code:

she awoke with answers
she could not tell her sisters.
But on her father's lap
one evening she explained

she would soon marry; Gerald,
the neighbor's son, lounged
with a conch to his pink ear:

what he heard was not the sea
but the hard, epic breathing
of a thin-lipped father.

5

Margaret, the youngest, flew
a kite, bright string and wings
flimsy as her own hair, red and
with ribbons—to the kite, a tail.

He was a father, but he knew
some day she would again need help
so he held an imaginary string,
he puffed till his cheeks bled.

Behind the man and girl on the hill
the sun descended. She hurried
to play enough, he hurried

for other, equally mysterious
reasons: each felt cold ascending
on dark wind like last breath.

Breakfast in the Suburbs

The enormous wife snipped the golden
stream of honey with her knife, turned
to the window to see a white poppy,
one petal missing, wave in the wind
a snaggletoothed smile. Butterflies
brush by in the rising morning heat.

She takes counsel with herself
like praying—she considers
the damages: two sisters,
two brothers, two parents.
Has anyone lived so symmetrically
as she? Two husbands, two
children, two cats (oh, when
will it end, the whole world
in twos like the senior prom,
and its madness to couple).

Her last husband had this,
the greatest grace of the sailor—
to tie knots and not to tangle.
But he was never home.

Sex Therapy

Autolycus, then, we discover, in the nineteenth book,
intended Odysseus to be a causer of pain.—G. R. Dimock, Jr.

The Weavings

The odor of gardens and of trees made the city
drowsy. In the apartments women watched
shapes flicker on television,

men became small memories of dinner cooking,
of beer bought on the way home,
or of laundry to be eventually done.

This wife worked winged horses, elephants rampant,
forsythia in bloom, green trees shaped like
popsicles, long flags

of imaginary wars in garish colors, all
with one needle. Sounds of announcers
waft into the sewing room, the news

of old wars. Some husband is always late
for something, or something grows cold
as dinner in any woman's life.

Telemachus

The moon as last ghost, pale as a pared fingernail,
Diana, or whatever is left of her in a secular age;
show whatever face it will

the moon, like grief, like a small yellow clock,
tells fabulous time, old, thus yellow, is nothing
but reflection.

He knows the woman whose window faces his;
he watches for a light, not moon, to show,
for a curtain ajar,

for what he knows of love to undress diaphanous
and slow, to turn and show appalling flesh
shiny as spoons;

he will let flow whatever, like tears,
will stain his fleshy,
dirty hand.

Calypso Sets Odysseus Free

An unwilling man with a willing woman. He
lit a cigarette and looked at the curve
of her back

at the glowing case of flesh which closes
over a butterfly-shaped bone. He thought:
It is all the same,

one night is as good as a wife. I will
go home and eat; at least I'm hungry.
He looked

at watery scarves draped on the furniture
like seaweed, at the curve of ceiling and shell-
shaped moulding

which made the room a cave; the sea
might have lapped at the windowsill; before
she awoke he left.

Nausicaä

Walking under his son's window he saw
the neighbor in her room; at the right angle
the voluptuous breast

shines through the night like a beacon
or moon, stops him. He stood for a time,
he looked.

As when a man goes to the summit and embraces
a naked wind and throws a rock over the precipice
so that the silence tells

the depth of possibility and he hopes with every
tendon straining to follow it, knowing the moment;
or when he looks

at the slender ribbon beneath the canyon rim shimmering
a dare to jump while the tourists watch horrified,
he looked again.

Polyphemus

Is this the father become the one-eyed monster, ugliest
of his race, eventually blind, full, to his son's
twisting mind,

of obscene intention? Even the amateur prophets know
the terrible rest and will tell all for only
a small fee;

these cook in the domestic kitchen: jealousy, lust,
anger and dissension, violence of flesh against
progenitive flesh.

This is the history of a strange subtle art,
the practice of cannibals called *parentage.* It yields
such stuff

that sons and daughters in search of lost fathers
for years will frantically dig through piles of flesh
called *marriage.*

The Sirens' Song

You can see their blue faces when they stand
beneath the street lights in groups of two or three.
Or you can see them in those thinly colored movies

copulating incessantly, mouthing some poor wretch's
witty lines (imagine, with some talent but no job,
writing the script—"something with a story,

not much to memorize"). Their nails are always
painted purple, or silver, or a searing shining blue.
And their bodies bear strange marks, small

significant scars. When the film jumps
and the sound goes you can hear the men breathing,
someone laughs, and we all hear a tearing tune,

something between those screams in the night
from your neighbor's house, and a whisper
swift as the bluish night.

Victory Drive, Near Fort Benning, Georgia

I hold a rattlesnake in my hand, gently:
even a bird does not have bones so fragile.
He is, in his way, humiliated, and makes
his rattle, his only poem. You can see him
any day, a lonely exhibit in a bar
where soldiers go to dream of jungles,
of chances lost.

Georgia

What bones? What bones? Stones instead.

I see a lamp hanging from a pickup truck,
two eager dogs, and men resting on stiff legs;

this state is filled with hunters, and frantic game
leaps fences, logs, the trees the roads the houses.

Yet only little violence, and mostly quiet: the shot
is seldom fired. The deer more likely dies

of scurrilous disease. The men wither dryly
as the corn in fall, then drift

over red horizons, become
the stone heart's surviving children,

remembered, boneless ghosts.

The Obscure Pleasure of the Indistinct

Under light soft as seawater, sounds
brush lightly past: shiver of laughter
from a pale woman's flimsy neck,
the rustle of linen under your own
hand resting on the table. You bite
into the dark meat of the pheasant,
you almost scream—you would,
were it not for your exquisite
parentage. Nestled in the stained
crevice of a molar a piece
of lead, shot, twice brutally painful:

and for a second time the bird flies
in your mind, and the long stiff
feathers brush the long brown leaf
on a cold autumn morning. Then
a sip of Pouilly-Fuisse, cool
on the tongue, soothing. Sounds
from the kitchen again are muffled, vague.

On Living the Rich, Full Life

He dreamed of dying witless, worn
completely, coughing
the last of his lungs as legacy.

Health like treasure he spent
discreetly on long nights
and short love, or longing

at seashores watching
young sailors, old whores,
the dreams of age, and ageless

he goes to his last bed knowing
nothing's left for nephews
natty in their Sunday suits dreaming

of vast fortune
forever gone, nothing
for lawyers but laughter.

Circus

Necromancers put their trust in their cercles, within which thei thinke them selfe sure against all ye devils in hel.
—Saint Thomas More, *A Dialoge Concerning Heresyes*

1

Small circle: cry O
among friends, among
forsythia in spring,
among stragglers
at the wedding
drunk on borrowed wine.

2

On the way to the beach
we watch hawks, points
in a perfect figure:
a long breath in the sun,
brutal epicycle, last
in a long line.

3

The widening longing
spiral at the funeral
culls last living relatives:
faint cousins from the mountains,
an uncle the boys
were warned against,
the red-haired nieces,
twelve in all—all
sit in a circle, wearing
knotted ties, dark suits,
some for the first, one
for the last time. Margaret,
who loved him best, stifles

a small cry, "O,"
and turns away.

    4

    The elegantly stupid
Afghan prepares for sleep
on my bed: I once counted
twelve complete circles, one
for each of her golden children.
Her nose softly punctuates
the line of her curving
tail; she sighs, then closes
her glorious eyes.

    5

    The world
of the suicide
the moment before
is zero, which is
not to say *nothing*,
but closed,
clean.

    6

    The plush dark
smell of water surrounded,

surrendered in a breath; we
hunted frogs, though I could,
I said, not eat them.
We wore lights;
we were armed with spears.
I still hear the delicate
thin skin tear, tight
across impossible bones.
On signal we extinguished
our lights and waited;
the warden's boat passed,
his bright disk of light
played ovals on the water,
wiped a clean half-moon
from shore to shore: a perfect
circle of fear surrounded me
like a saint's halo.

7

The moon plays
its variations on circle:
a radial lung it breathes
light.

8

So the children
of the light sing Holy

Holy Holy Lord God of Hosts,
holding their open mouths
like the golden lips of fish
in an old lake depleted
of oxygen and of hope;
they flap elbows or gills
in the muted light, sun
shining on the golden vanity
of children as of fish,
an old prehensile cycle.

9

I sat with the pilot.
I watched where I knew propellers were,
then we descended into rain
somewhere over Florida, and I saw
a delicate, gray, soft circle—
I thought: the world is large
enough; somewhere
it is not raining, somewhere
it is not Florida. Then we landed
so softly the wheels
whispered no answer.

10

In this quiet
valley red by last

light, last heat warming
him, the indigo snake
steals eggs. What
a small adventure,
this little O,
his meal now a bulge,
glistening scales
like a cancer.
Haunted by legend
and the mother bird
(*Rallus limicola*, orange
beak, eye circled by white)
the snake is often hated,
was thought to make itself
a wheel to escape
tail in mouth downhill.
He will sleep three days
digesting one
entire generation.

11

The flung
spray in the rich man's lawn,
the pinwheel sprinkler in June,
silver artillery, sprung-spiral,
dances. Meanwhile
in the deep house, back
in the shadows of this green,

behind the small rainbows,
a woman contemplates adultery.
But no young man braves
the machine-gun-sound
of the sprinklers, not
to mention the doberman
asleep in the sun, not
for any brass ring.

12

Some child traces a circle
on a windowpane. The fine rain
trickles silent as the purest crying.
As she retraces the figure a thin
whine, as of the blood, fills
her ear full as the sound
of surf in a pink shell.
As you quietly close the door
to leave her undisturbed
she turns too quickly.
You see the look
in her desolate eye.

Rose Hill Shopping Center

It broods beneath glister of evening rain
*   under slender light posts*
Waiting—a wife in a raincoat, a fling
*   of wet hair—lost and lingering.*

Junior's Crafts

The place shimmers with birds after
    the storm: parking lot, roof,
Any surface fills with feathers.
    The rain rises from car hoods;

The birds have picked all available
    drowned worms. A magnolia
Drips an agony of green. The last
    puff quivers across

Two linked puddles. Junior
    looks at this from the door.
He didn't sleep well. Each waking
    changes your life—the world

Is strange each time the dog barks,
    the train rattles the window,
Or the drips from the bathroom accumulate
    till you sit up in bed.

Junior remembers his childhood, remembers
    mainly waiting. His father
Was always late. The boys were gone
    from the game, but Junior

Would watch the fireflies on the basepaths,
    would watch the neighboring
Houses, each window glow orange.
    Sometimes he'd count stars.

Drug Store

Large lewd man, sitting on a stool,
    tells his story to a friend,
The friend recently divorced, lonely,
    listening silent, alert:

When my daughter was born I
    was there, saw her nails
Needed cutting, and she had no hair.
    Shocked to scream

She lay in a kind of nest they made
    on Lou's belly (slack
And still disappointing) and stared
    at me. We'd never get on

With this start, I said to myself,
    this is no way to begin.
That night I kissed Lou, left
    for home with a nurse who tore

The bed to shreds—she knew her stuff—
    and cried to think I did
Such things, me a family man.
    Get out while you can.

Estelle's Piano Studio

If the Gulf Oil moon can peer through bare
    branches this purple evening,
Then why not bees buzzing about the sticky
    lip of a Coke bottle?

North of here forests as virginal pine
    as you'll find in this state
Shiver across mountains hiding
    veins of quick water.

Estelle, proprietress, shuffles paper:
    she has students enough
To pay the rent; she sold two organs
    this month. She has cried

Three times since childhood: once
    for the death of a husband,
Once for a dog, and this morning for no
    reason—she was looking

Across the parking lot, her vision wavered
    in heat. She was thinking of Mozart,
Of home, and of children's stubby fat
    fingers—she was thinking of luck.

Laundromat

A politician's wellspring. To the right
    as you enter enclosed
In glass is his office. He ran from there
    his campaign for congress while rising

To run to balance loads for women
    with quilts and bedspreads. He looks
Often, now a senator, across
    his dream fulfilling, seamless

Blue of ceiling, chief of the white
    wash of women, their slips,
Their blouses, their husbands' shorts, the sheets
    off their very beds.

And the threat, the Menace he lives
    on, off of, the Reds.
What strange power burgeons in bed
    fellows, what passionate politics

Fills the speeches he makes when the money
    is safe in the banks,
The doors to the laundromat locked. Children
    can sleep in clean linen.

Big Ed's Hair Stylist

What you first notice, next to Big Ed,
   is the Free Take One
Bible Story rack on the wall.
   Complete Beauty Work

And God at one convenient location.
   He is sad and loud.
A girl shampoos and does the rare
   manicure. He doesn't

Believe in fairies. He whispers a dream:
   there were wisps of wind
Winding to the sea, a few that looked
   like miles of laundry,

Clouds, and the face of God set
   like the sun. My children
Loved me again, and men off
   in the blue distance waved,

Their friendly faces wide, heads
   shaggy as sheep dogs.
I heard them calling for me, the last
   lonely barber, needed.

Bubba's Flowers and Gifts

When Bubba worked for his mother across
    town, he might search
Through the files for hours (under *D*
    for "Dishes") for china which brides

In clumsy innocence chose. Now
    his shop is his own. He doesn't
Do brides. His mother taught him all
    he knows, gave him all

She owned. Before she retired she told
    him about his father,
How they met in New York—he followed
    her from the steps

Of The Plaza until, crying, delicately,
    she said: Have you
No shame? And he said: No. And she
    followed him home

To his farm: *There were pastures where*
    your father took me,
Across the road. I sat with his mother
    breaking bean pods

Pulling green strings, breaking
    fingernails, and would watch
Cows wade among the birds which lived
    on ticks. For three years

I lived with birds' song and sun,
*   the seed ripped in birds'*
Beaks and the clatter of husk to the porch
*   floor. The feeder, the porch,*

The blue shadows, the twining scarlet
*   pimpernel, and at a far*
Corner, you playing, drooling
*   on a towel. You never*

Knew your father, but I can tell
*   you this: he made such*
A beautiful corpse, and the flowers
*   inspired us all.*

The Late Show

There
Is just so much nothing you can bear
Waiting.

1

The movie's in black and white but
the commercials are in color. Sad
men in southern accents sell
tiny Japanese cars to Veterans
of Foreign Wars; women show us
our enormous-breasted daughters
with business school certificates.

A man named Warren watches as if
his sleeping son were on the screen.
He, like anyone, has things to do
but doesn't do them; Bette Davis loves
ecstatic in his stead. A sudden
crack—the ice shifts in his forgotten glass.

2

He sees his only son ramble among
the crumbling ruins of a garden,
eating the oranges sprung spindly
from seed, crushing the wild rose
beneath his boots, scaring chameleons

from the warm smooth breast
of a fallen Venus. He holds
his own bright party beneath the trees.

He knows, dream or not, nothing
of the dead beneath him, the rotting
roots and bones bared to the translating
microbes; the garden is in Italy
and if the dream shifted to winter
the pool would glaze with ice and save
its one remaining goldfish from his
impetuous flung stones.

3

Warren wakes; his neck hurts.
The softly sifting snow
crackles across the screen.

No one in the waking world loves
his shuffling movement toward
the television; no one brushes
his hand with her soft lips as
it reaches for the button;
no one saves for him the gold
light which filled the one room
he dreadfully darkens.

The Petting Zoo

Imagine my first son dreams of the sheep
he first touched today, neither he nor they
yet one year old. He dreams in his snugness
of bed surrounded by damp breath and urine,
still a comfort to his ignorance,
of the oily gray cloud shocking hard
shell of sheep: such wool pulled
over his tiny eyes! He still loves
only himself mirrored in his world;
his touch, not theirs, thrills him.
He knows nothing, not
the use of lamb's intestines for condoms;
not the use of lanolin to smooth
his own raw buttocks; nor of the wool
in his blanket, nor the money I paid
to the greasy young man, bored past greed,
keeper of that pathetic, tired collection.
The sun beat into our eyes as we left.

I pushed his fine-boned body
in the spindly aluminum carriage
and I noticed him notice the smell
still there on his hand, the smell
of a world he still didn't know
wasn't him, though he perhaps began
to suspect the membrane—thinly
stretched as vellum—through which
no one can reach, nor no star shine.

Butterflies, Late Fall: Nostalgia

Returning and returning we clip
the wings of a hundred Sulphurs;
they festoon the grills of cars as if
it's homecoming and our school color yellow.

For a month the rain delayed them;
now under sun they ascend buttery,
slippery in wind in the wake of cars
on the interstate. I listen to my old school

lose on the radio while I smash
their slight formation.
I watch in the mirror the swirl
of littered bodies, kite-thin lives like laughter.

III

Mater Dolorosa

1

Pollen from the goldenrod rises
to the power lines. On wet days
a crackle echoes among pylons
frightening the cows: but this
morning, cold, dry, and gold,
you hear a faint hiss as if
from electric flowers.

My mother, at the dining room window,
sighs for the passing of power above her,
and for time, and for one more season.

*

For each of my sins she cried,
but that is the duty of mothers.

2

In Italy the rainwater drains
through a sluice in the garden wall.
A young man, slightly drunk,
steps delicately across the puddle
moving in the road below.
He thinks how his mother
before he wakes will clean his shoes
then not speak for three days.

*

In the terminal in Texas
we sit drinking coffee, waiting;
we look at an airline poster of Montreal,
the city lighted at night,
and we say we would live there

if we could live only there,
among the lights and lucent air,
far above the streets. Or that
is what I say; my mother says:
It is late; your father
flies through bad weather.

3

I have her eyes, they say, and so
I turn away. I often close
our secret eyes.

Rain

Again a dreariness beyond belief:
the boy begins to contemplate,
in Saturday's rain, late autumn,
adultery. He doesn't know it
but it shimmers from his lamp
in the semi-mirrored window.

He remembers summer and his striped
beach chair. From behind him
you would have seen the sway
of beach grass, and his yellow
cap flaring his talented ears.
The head, close-cut hair,
and a few inches of chair float
on those grassy waves before you.

He observed—a boy's delinquency—
a most magnificent sun descend:
orange, green glints in the few clouds,
a bird or two blackened calling
as if pitying him
his protruding ears.
Then a woman

breasts bare against the cooling,
against the going sun, walks
against the gold-capped waves
streaming her bikini in one hand.

He held his breath
then hotly breathed:

I never suspected,
I never suspected so round.

Now, the cold comes back, the beach
groans miles away. And in this rain
he cries and cruelly dreams,
(oh sly and sentimental boy),
of a glint of flesh in last light.

What to Do Till the Doctor Comes

People live here . . . you'd be amazed.—Louis Simpson

1

I am looking for a woman who reads Chekhov
and has green eyes and has been known
to cry while making love. I, for my part,
like onions and always burp
three times after dinner.
She must not try to change me.

2

Because there are green leaves falling,
even in spring time,
because some men play football on Saturdays
even after they are fifty-two years old,
because some children sit on front porches
watching moths flicker around street lights,
because some girls laugh, a bit too loudly,
on the way home from the library,
a man in our town has murdered seven old women,
strangled them with their own stockings, after doing
strange things with a broom handle.

3

So go on and tell me about love
and how you have written to her
every day for three weeks since she left
for Saint Louis. I know that she loves you
even if she cannot, quite, remember your name.
It could happen to anyone.

Drive-in

Its rigid vigil of speaker and post
touches history more surely
than any Arlington's skeletal crosses
mute in all weather.
In Ohio, five miles east
of Athens, we knew summer would return,
an old message would be told
in the season's pictures.

Someone died there ten years ago:
I saw it, then the next night he returned
to die again. He died for love,
of which money is only
one of many forms. He died for us
and we loved for him, listening
while coupling in back seats.

Remember that Alan Ladd
taught us something by dying;
maybe it was dignity,
though he had to stand on a box
to do it tall enough.

The Dangers of the Domestic

I know her face locked in sleep
and the sound of her teeth grinding
exceeding fine. How sad it is
to analyze a wife sleeping, to ask
whatever questions fit
her random answers.
She speaks from the pillow
in feathery tongues.

Her teeth will go bad by forty;
they consume themselves all night.
I have wakened to their gnashing—
agony speaks louder than love.

I do not know if in the refrigerator
a light like a Berkeleyan vision
burns in cold security; doors
and eyes closed at night
keep us guessing:

what we love is not a husband, not a wife;
we love the frosty grandeur of our ignorance,
we love our smaller secrets and our sleep.

Foreign Language

Try to remember the sound of the sea,
the wash of amnion on a shell-like ear.
At dinner tonight the oysters were good
but the taste of salt lingers.
Wine subdued all moderation
while talk faded into the wallpaper.

As she answered I imagined
the umbilical mariner, infinitely old,
infinite regress of self, intimate
with women—the embryo I was
is dead. What else could memory dredge
from reluctant mothers?

    *

After dinner we talked in the garden.
The dogwood glowed above us in the light
spilled from the living room, the jasmine
insinuated between us its thick smell
sexual, unforgiving. You made a gesture.

Between men and women some words work,
but very few. I have heard the French
speak them, and once an Italian,
but that was long ago
and in the movies.

Meanwhile I remain in the garden
beneath the dogwood:

what I said was well intentioned
but unforgivable. To love well
is to remember little. We will someday
forget everything—we will marry,
you will have children. I
will ask them what it was like,
and they will eat oysters, drink wine,
and whisper as I leave the room.

*

Once I saw a woman gleam
after a swim in the ocean at night.
She spoke softly to herself, picked up
her basket and walked toward me.

Saint Anthony Confronts Sodomy in the New World

Refined out of childhood,
a crystalline porch I stepped delicately
over into the house,
into the dark kitchen called adolescence,

I, a self-made boy, fraught
with implication, called the name obscener
than the act. The scene, as if engraved
on glass, is there, but must be focused on
accurately or it reverts
to background:

I recall how dreadfully
I went when visiting
my cousin's house. We slept
doubled in his room; late
alone with him he
made me hold him,
he made me. What a large hand-
full he was, and I did not
know its name: enormous stars
outside billowed lightly
like clean sheets hiding
an infinite disease.

Nuns in Sunshine

1

High above, he pitched a tent for the sun,
who comes out of his pavilion like a bridegroom,
exulting like a hero to run his race. Psalm 19:5.

2

I was privileged to know them
in their full habitual splendor
striding through classrooms
winged and wafting the sharp-
edged smell of starch,
black and white as the answers
in the Baltimore Catechism.

3

Walking in our own mirage, shimmering,
a hundred degrees, we picked
blackberries beside the black road.

The barbed wire of the fence
was no harder than the thorns, less sharp.
The male plants stood stiff,
barren, the bearing vines twined.

It is hard to remember surviving
childhood in Texas, the heat: it's hell,

they said gleefully, on women and horses.
But think of the nuns!

    4

Six irises in a blue vase—
green swords of leaves
and stems thick as pointed fingers:
Sister Francesca arranges them
against the white wall of the chapel,
the passion of pistil and stamen
beneath her fingers, and the hushed
hiss of wind winds through the pews.

    5

A picnic for the end of school,
nuns in summer starch and beads
fly down the basepaths.

Twelve of the girls are in love
with Sister Francesca:

they tell each other stories
of a lover in New Orleans
who waits in bitter silence

for her return, her renunciation
of vows. There is such a look

in the girls' eyes I do not laugh.
I watch Sister Francesca lean
toward second base; small breezes

lift her balancing arm's sleeve—
I see further white,

like my grandfather's long
underwear. Yet I still
don't laugh. Lovers.

Her hair never again to lighten
under the sun. The sun

burned my eyes when she moved
on invisible legs away,
her side striking out.

Three Views of One Woman

"Any clear thing that blinds us with surprise"
—Robert Lowell

1

I watched a woman wake today: the sun
touched that point the sideways bone
makes in her shoulder. She moved from glory
to the bathroom. She looked into my eyes
trying to remember her last long dream.

What is the place of pity in a dream?
Watch for it, it wells up from
the dark places like lint
coiled in our bathrobe pockets.

Break against it like salmon, like anything
on a short string, to jump time
and time again until the snap
and you leap, twisting over the fall.

2

New light long angled through a wide
window sweeps across her: she sleeps.
I touch her cheek, a spot I know
will rouse her. She will not
remember.

The day is ruined, her dream unfinished.
She pulls the strap back over her shoulder—
the glimpse of nipple covered, passion
spent.

The color of nipple, the color
of the sun rising: salmon. I lie
in bed while the sounds of water seep
from the bathroom—

it is worse to marry *and* to burn.
I turn, twisting sheets, to sleep
a little longer.

3

Perversion, past redemption, awakened
by first light and useless
twitter of birds in slight sun;
embarrassed in bed I watch her sleep.

Her gown is coiled tight
against that expensive
thigh: the bulge, exuberant
of sex, false promise,
flesh.

We would once wake twisting
into each other—like vines
blooming on a fence post, like
strands of barbed wire, like
two caught eels in one net,
like twisted bread dough

rising, like any girl's
last illusion.

The whole day lies
in her fist,
tight, puffed
as her crusted eyes,
which I slyly kiss open.

What We Learned to Do to Each Other

Early enough, long past the comfort
of darkness, at the time when gray
outlines hiss into the room, she sat up
to watch the window in the mirror.

The plaster stuck solid to the ceiling.
His slow breathing coiled about
her shoulders; she shivered.
The mist in the mirror seemed

For a moment to clear, then move
voluminously beyond.
The baby cried and she put on
her robe and woke her husband.

The next morning it happened again,
and the next, and the next.

The Rape of the Divorcée's Sisters

1

On the corner of Thirteenth and Cedar
a dark fountain splashes in the rain.
The street light forces
an occasional glitter, a scintillant drop
against the farther gray. No figure walks
stooped against cold or rain.

If the world grows dim around us
it has its reasons: absence is its own reward.
Some Napoleon even now plots Waterloo
behind dim-lit panes; a woman
draws a thin curtain slightly aside,
looks at the splash of fountain, hears
the rain, then turns; the curtain falls
back as she sips her chocolate.

2

"I am sick of your silly solitude—who
are you to be happy?"

(Do you hear my father speak? Oh,
he is taller and younger than I,
he is blond and has thirty women
lining his driveway as he leaves
for the office.)

"Join my firm and work; join
a club; have more babies."

(It is the duty of fathers never
to lack for advice. It is the duty
of fathers to scold. It is the duty
of sons to marry.)

"Give to charity; exercise regularly;
invest at no less than six percent."

(But I, too, am a father; I fell
for all his tricks. I move to the window
to watch for rain as I tell my son
how to pay for the sins
visited upon his dear
blond head.)

3

The sisters come—
not cheerily bearing gifts
through the drizzling rain, not strewing
petals of poppy to my empty bed—
they come reluctantly, bitterly asking:
"If you loved her, why send her away?
If you did not love, why keep her
till all was lost?" Then
they lie down, white lipped, crying,
to let me have, once more, my way.

Through the dripping window
beside my bed I watch the splash

of dark water flecked
with yellow light, the fountain
in slow rain. There is no
small woman there, huddled
under the coat I gave her
seven years ago, watching
the slow dissolution of this, our own,
our only world.

Pleasures of the Flesh

I watch her in the morning look
at three birds brooding on a wire
like suicides on a ledge.
She knows its uselessness,
how she would only spread wings
to save herself at the last moment.

Sadness is neither virtue nor vice,
though it has caused music,
and flowers, and pathetic smiles
to line the long highways of our state.

Evening Seduction Scene with Telescope

Use dusky words and dusky images,
Darken your speech.　　　—Wallace Stevens

Like a slow sheet settling
on a making bed, dark
pigeons waft themselves
to roost;

this end of the day there arises
the passion to hear secrets
full of false sibilants
in a shadowy room:

"This evening star, Mars,
through the telescope looks
like a fertile egg—see
those streaks like blood?"

*

Once I was young
and read novels and thought:
some men wear silk bathrobes
and carry home women under
one arm, French bread under
the other. But I will always
grope in the dark hoping
to touch something soft.

(It is probably not good to recall
the dark self-pity, better to remember
football, bones broken in passionate
victory, even if it never happened.)

90

At night I would wander
window to window, the household
asleep, and I'd look at stars,
draw imaginary lines, connect
the dots. Eventually I'd go
to bed.

    *

He swings the brass eyepiece
smoothly as *terra firma*
on its axis toward her.
He delicately holds her waist
as she looks. She asks
"Why isn't it Venus?"

    *

Beneath a window in the late
summer darkness, white
violets—contradiction, and faint
ghost of odor—sprinkle themselves
in the dew like reflections
of stars, or of the last light
in the house, forgotten on.

The Desire for a Mediterranean Sea

In a perfect gesture of defeat a boy
Turns a water pistol to his mouth
And tastes the metallic sting of spray.

I have always lived in lands of hot
Weather and wetness. Today I watched
From the library portico the rain

Glitter into the hair of students
While children at home, pistols
Drawn and dripping, dreamed

Of dry afternoons and cool green
Lawns filled with cats worth soaking.
Il pleure dans mon cœur

Comme il pleut sur la ville.
Quelle est cette langueur
Qui pénètre mon cœur?

That afternoon in Louisiana a woman
With an accent talked of home, France,
And the color of roses cascading

Into the windows of cars,
Windows open to the breeze off
The Mediterranean, across the sand.

As she talked the shapes of billowing
Curtains in the room changed from shy
To aggressive, from simpering to querulous,

And back again in soft cycles. And shapes
Of oceans, as I watched and listened, opened
Ragged windows, wind-eyes, wide

Shapes of the exotic lives lost
That might have been mine. Wet
Processions in Venice hiss

Across stones worn by wind
And rain and tourists' feet while a child
Takes deadly aim wetly.

Travelogue
  for Richard Hugo

The cut edge of decanter reflects
first sun and last streetlight:
amber of whiskey and bitter dreams
conspire to make us go, or, sometimes, stay.

1

I stood in a house on a hill,
its own hill, all hundred acres,
abandoned in 1947.
Fleas infested the carpets. Two wings
and a view of two states, one Alabama.
A villa of sorts, a mansion, post-war
but *influenced*. A friend will live there
with its curves of bannisters
like mirrored seashells, its marble mouths
of fireplaces, its sultry ghosts
and bad plumbing.

Otherwise there is nothing to do
in this city, and no place to go.

2

I have never been to Italy but this
is what it's like: stone upon stone
and sunlight, but mainly you ride
a Maserati convertible on Roman

94

Legions' roads while tall cypresses,
regular as telephone poles,
whiz over your left shoulder.

And late evening sun spills
wine-like over the tops of ruins
while you make designs on the table
with the condensation from your glass.
And one evening a woman speaks
three words into your ear, and if
you smile, she leads you
up stone stairs to a room
full of stars and open windows.

Dwells with me still mine irksome *Memory*,
Which, both to keepe, and lose, grieves equally.
—John Donne, *Heroicall Epistle*